595

AF411753

WIMBLEDON
WORLD TENNIS FOCUS

By JULIAN MAY

Creative Education
Mankato, Minnesota

Photograph and Illustration Credits

ILLUSTRATORS

John Keely, Minneapolis 10, 14, 19

PHOTOGRAPHERS

UPI 1, 11, 12, 13, 17, 21, 23, 25,
27, 28, 29, 34, 37, 43, 45
Wide World Photos 2, 31, 42
"Acme" 15, 16
Ralph Guillumette 6

Published by Creative Educational Society, Inc., 123 South Broad Street,
Mankato, Minnesota 56001. Copyright © 1975 by Creative Educational
Society, Inc. International copyrights reserved in all countries.
No part of this book may be reproduced in any form without written
permission from the publisher. Printed in the United States.
Distributed by Childrens Press, 1224 West Van Buren Street, Chicago,
Illinois 60607.
Library of Congress Number: 75-17779   ISBN: 0-87191-444-1
Library of Congress Cataloging in Publication Data

May, Julian.   Wimbledon.
   (Sports classic)
   SUMMARY: A brief history of the world champion tennis
tournament at Wimbledon, with brief sketches of some of
its singles champions.
   1. Tennis—Biography—Juvenile literature. 2. All-England
Club, Wimbledon, Eng.—Juvenile literature.
(1. Tennis—Biography.   2. All-England Club,
Wimbledon, Eng.)   I. Title.
GV994.A1M38   796.34'2'0922   (B)   (920)   75-17779
ISBN o-87191-444-1

Contents

The famous Centre Court at Wimbledon, where the finals are played, becomes the focus of world tennis interest each summer.

All-England, All-World

Who are the world champion tennis players?

To most tennis fans, the best players of the year are those who win the Singles finals at Wimbledon in England. A woman or man may win other tennis tournaments elsewhere. But no contest means as much as Wimbledon. It is the world championship of tennis.

Every summer, the top players from all over the world come to England. The actual name of the tournament is the All-England Championships. It is held at the All-England Lawn Tennis and Croquet Club, Wimbledon, London.

The Club is very beautiful. It has green lawns, roses, ivy, and stately rows of pink and blue flowers. It has shaded tables where people can eat strawberries and cream. It has tennis courts with pelts of special grass, coddled like orchids.

There are many courts at Wimbledon. But the focus of all attention is Centre Court. Here the finals are played. Here is the Royal Box reserved for English nobility. Here are the largest grandstands.

Here is the world's greatest tennis challenge.

Stars of Centre Court

The world's oldest tennis championship match was first played at Wimbledon in 1877. The players were all men, all English, and all amateurs. Both players and spectators were members of the upper class.

They had dignity.

In 1884, ladies in long skirts began to skip over the grass courts. They wore large hats and were careful not to show their ankles.

It was the time of Queen Victoria. Proper behavior was almost the most important thing in the lives of the English upper class. Tennis, being an upper-class game, had to be proper and dignified, too. The game acquired a tradition of stuffiness and snobbery. This would cling to it through the years.

Fortunately, the game and the Wimbledon contest were too exciting to be smothered. The proper English would be shocked again and again by the terrible things that *some* players (foreigners, of course) would do.

Take the first American girl to win Women's Singles — 18-year-old May Sutton. She rolled up her sleeves to play! Miss Sutton won in 1905 and 1907.

The men were even worse. Irishmen, Americans, and players from Australia and New Zealand invaded Wimbledon. The outlanders were hard-driving and tough. They licked the British champions, who favored pitty-pat service and a cautious, polite style. But these foreigners also made the game exciting. Royalty began to attend. When a Royal

Suzanne Lenglen was said to be "effortless as a lioness." Her accuracy was fantastic and many critics have called her the best woman player of all. She was not beautiful, but her charm, talent, and grace of movement made her the most renowned player of her time. Lenglen was champion in 1919, 1920, 1921, 1922, 1923, and 1925.

Person watched, the players would bow before beginning.

After World War I, a new freedom swept through the world of sport. The most exciting Wimbledon champion was a Frenchwoman, Suzanne Lenglen. She beat the legendary Mrs. Lambert Chambers, seven times a winner. And the way she did it shocked and delighted England.

Lenglen sneered at long skirts and petticoats. She was French, she was chic, she was an athlete. She did the sensible thing and played in knickers and a breezy dress that was nearly transparent.

Shocking! The proper British flocked to watch her play. She won the Women's Singles six times.

Britain's greatest woman champion was Dorothea Douglass Lambert Chambers. She won the Singles seven times between 1903 and 1914. She is shown here in 1925 after she gave up her long skirts and petticoats for more modern tennis garb.

Dashing Frenchmen, dubbed the "Musketeers," dominated Wimbledon Men's Singles during the 1920's. At left is Rene Lacoste (champion in 1925 and 1928). His opponent here is Henri Cochet (champion in 1927 and 1929). The third "Musketeer" was Jean Borotra, who won in 1924 and 1926.

In 1920 and 1921, a tall American named William T. Tilden II starred in Centre Court. He was the first Yankee to take the Men's Singles. Tilden was one of the most powerful players of all. His serve was said to exceed 124 mph!

Lenglen and Tilden attracted such large crowds that the tournament had to move. It went to larger quarters in 1922. The King and Queen opened the new Wimbledon.

In the mid-1920's three French "Musketeers" named Jean Borotra, Rene Lacoste, and Henri Cochet grabbed Wimbledon glory away from Tilden. But he kept trying to win. And in 1930, Tilden was again world champion.

The Two Helens

The woman destined to take the place of Suzanne Lenglen was a different kind of tennis queen. Young Helen Wills was called "Little Miss Poker Face." She was as calm as Lenglen was fiery. Helen played a classic baseline game of great power. Her trademark was a white eyeshade.

Helen Wills won the Women's Singles at Wimbledon in 1927 and 1928. The next year, she defeated another Helen who would become her greatest rival.

Helen Hull Jacobs was also an American and

Helen Wills Moody was nine-times queen of Wimbledon. She won the Women's Singles in 1927, 1928, 1929, 1930, 1932, 1933, 1935, and 1938. Her record is unequalled.

Helen Hull Jacobs won Wimbledon in 1936 and was five times a runner-up. She won the U.S. championship four times.

also from Berkeley, California. Unlike the other Helen, she was a volleyer and a net-rusher. The tennis press concocted a "feud" between the two women. In 1932, Helen Wills Moody beat Helen Jacobs again. Then Moody's game seemed to weaken. She lost to Jacobs at Forest Hills by default in 1933. Both women came to Wimbledon the next year in a rather grim mood.

Moody played fiercely to regain her crown and prestige. In one of the most thrilling matches yet seen, she beat Jacobs 6-3, 3-6, 7-5. It was her seventh Wimbledon title.

Helen Jacobs won Wimbledon in 1936, playing against Hilda Krahwinkel Sperling. There would be one last contest against Helen Wills Moody, in 1938. And once again, Helen Jacobs would finish second-best. She herself always denied that there was any feud between her and Helen Wills Moody. Her good sportsmanship was legendary.

Don vs. The Baron

Baron Gottfriend von Cramm *(left)* was Germany's greatest male player. He had lost the Wimbledon Men's Singles finals twice to Frederick J. Perry of Britain before meeting Don Budge *(right)* in 1937. Von Cramm's anti-Nazi attitudes caused his persecution by Hitler. After World War II, he returned to tennis as a beloved senior player.

In the '30's, the image of tennis as a rich man's game was starting to crumble. One of the greatest and most modest of male champions helped attract ordinary people to the game. His name was Don Budge.

The son of a laundry manager, he learned his game on the public courts of Oakland, California. He was a gangling redhead, anything but graceful. But his all-court game was a miracle of power. In 1936, when he was 20, he was ranked number one in the U.S.

Next year, he came undefeated to Wimbledon. He had helped America win back the Davis Cup. Budge's opponent in the Wimbledon finals was a player of the old school. Baron Gottfried von Cramm was a German aristocrat, as charming and stylish as a movie star. His game was elegant. Some people called it beautiful.

Budge nearly lost his nerve in the finals. He had to keep telling himself, "Hold your serve, Budge!" Quaking inside, he was still able to defeat the Baron after coming from behind to win the fifth set.

Strangely enough, von Cramm and Don Budge became friends. They played for the U.S. tennis championship at Forest Hills later in 1937. In another exciting battle of the giants, Budge won in three sets out of five.

The next year, Don Budge became the first man to win tennis' Grand Slam — Wimbledon, Forest Hills, and the French and Australian titles. Then he turned pro and was lost to Wimbledon play.

The day was coming when the sacred rule of all-amateur play at Wimbledon would be set aside. But such an idea was too shocking in 1938.

Very Mixed Doubles

In 1939, two American players — Alice Marble and Bobby Riggs — took the Wimbledon Singles titles. They also won the Mixed Doubles that year.

More than 30 years later, both players would greatly influence the career of another champion, Billie Jean King.

Alice Marble was tall, blonde, and powerful. She had a bullet-like serve and liked to volley. Her game was widely compared to that of a man. She played in a sensible cap and shorts — very shocking!

Marble first attained renown in 1936 when she won the American championship from Helen Jacobs. Alice's triumph came after she overcame a long illness that had nearly ended her career. She was destined to win the American title three more times besides taking Wimbledon in 1939. World War II put an end to any further attempts. After doing volunteer war work, she became a professional player and a singer. She also taught the young Billie Jean King, whose style greatly resembled that of Marble herself.

In his later years, Bobby Riggs became a tennis hustler and figure of fun. His defeat by Billie Jean King (after he had whipped Margaret Court)

Bobby Riggs at Wimbledon in 1939. He was a master of the controlled game during an era of "big hitting." Often underrated, he was respected by tennis greats such as Don Budge (whom he beat in the 1946 pro finals). Big Bill Tilden said he was one of the best defensive players of all.

brought a blaze of publicity to tennis and to Riggs himself.

But few people who watched the King-Riggs match knew of Bobby Riggs' glorious early career. He was a short, catlike man with a deceiving service. He was 21 when he won not only Wimbledon but also Forest Hills.

Bobby Riggs was clever and ambitious. He wanted to make money playing tennis, and the only way to do that was to turn pro. The pros who made the most were those who had won many championships. The war put an end to Wimbledon. (Bombs damaged the club and pigs were raised on the sacred turf!) Bobby Riggs had to make his reputation in the United States.

He reached the finals at Forest Hills in 1940, but lost narrowly to Don McNeill. Next year, Riggs did capture the U.S. Men's title. But the war came to the United States and his hopes for a pro career were dashed.

After the war, Riggs resumed his pro career. Big money escaped him. But he kept trying.

In 1971, when he was 53, he challenged U.S. Champion Billie Jean King to a "man *vs.* woman" match. She turned him down. Still hoping to exploit the women's lib theme, he played against three-time Wimbledon winner Margaret Smith Court, beating her on Mother's Day, 1973.

Billie Jean King agreed to play him later that year. After trading humorous insults, the two played a serious game of tennis. A gallery of 30,000 — largest ever — watched, while millions more watched on TV. They saw King murder Riggs, 6-4, 6-3, 6-3.

Bobby Riggs and Billie Jean King meet at a press conference before their famous match. Riggs had maintained that he could beat any woman — even though he was old and out of shape. He claimed that women could not bear up under pressure.

The Immortal Gussie

When World War II ended, Wimbledon was rebuilt, more beautiful than ever. The championships resumed in 1946. Men's tennis was livened by the electric Jack Kramer, an American who took the title in 1947.

But postwar women's tennis was drab — until the big fuss about proper tennis attire!

A designer named Teddy Tinling had been making women's tennis garb for years. After the war, some women asked for touches of color — and got them. The result was disapproving headlines in the press.

When English champion Betty Hilton lost to Louise Brough in 1948, the defeat was blamed on Hilton's dress. It sported a naughty band of color, instead of being regulation white.

In 1949, the biggest scandal of all broke out. Gussie Moran, a high-ranking American girl, wore a short skirt with lace-trimmed panties that showed.

The crowd gaped. Ministers preached sermons against Moran's tennis clothes. Newspapers all over the world put her picture on the front page. People who had never cared about women's tennis before became interested.

The fuss was almost as great as that over the Billie Jean King-Bobby Riggs match 24 years later. And the result was the same — priceless publicity for tennis and for Wimbledon.

Gussie Moran never won the world championship. But Wimbledon never forgot her.

Gertrude (Gussie) Moran wearing the costume
that gave Wimbledon one of its biggest shocks
in 1949.

Stars Of Mid-Century

The middle decades of the 20th century saw the rise of colorful tennis champions. There was Louise Brough, one of the greatest woman athletes, who won Wimbledon's Women's Singles four times and was runner up three times.

There was Richard A. (Pancho) Gonzales, a handsome, explosive player of unbending pride. Born in Los Angeles of Mexican-American parents, he became an expert player without ever having a pro lesson. Tennis snobs in California tried to ban him from competition because he had not finished high school. Pancho fought this ruling and won. He won the U.S. championship in 1948 at the age of 19 and has continued to be an exciting and popular player into the 1970's.

There was Maureen (Little Mo) Connolly, a cool, relentless "killer" of a player who won the Singles three times in a row (1952-54). Many have ranked her above Suzanne Lenglen. Her brief career

Pancho Gonzales at Wimbledon in 1969. He beat Sweden's Ove Bengtsson in a preliminary match, but did not reach the finals. Gonzales is one of Wimbledon's most famous also-rans in the singles. He won the Men's Doubles with Frank Parker in 1949, the U.S. title in 1948 and 1949, and was Pro Champion in 1954, 1955, 1956, 1957, 1958, 1959, 1960, and 1961.

Maureen Connolly *(left)* defeated Louise Brough *(right)* in 1952 at the age of 17, becoming the youngest woman to win Wimbledon since 1887. (In that year, an English girl named Lottie Dod took the event at the age of 15.) Connolly was the first woman to win the Grand Slam of tennis — in 1953. Louis Brough won the Singles in 1948, 1949, and 1950. In 1955, after Connolly retired, Brough won again.

Althea Gibson came from the sidewalks of Harlem to the manicured lawns of Wimbledon. She had to fight prejudice every step of the way. People such as Alice Marble helped force the tennis establishment to give Gibson her chance. After overcoming many setbacks, she won Wimbledon in 1957 and 1958.

was cut tragically short by an accident that injured her leg in 1954, when she was only 20 years old.

There was Jaroslav Drobny, first a Czech, then a man without a country, who tried for 11 years to win Wimbledon. A sentimental favorite, he finally won the big title in 1954 as thousands cheered and wept.

There was Lew Hoad, the "Big Australian," two-time Wimbledon winner. There was Althea Gibson, the first black woman to become a tennis champion, who won both the U.S. and Wimbledon titles in 1957 and 1958.

All brought new glory to tennis.

Jaroslav Drobny reached the Wimbledon semi-finals six times and the finals three times before finally winning the Singles in 1954. "Old Drob," a beloved Centre Court figure, was an ancient 32 at the time of his victory. He and Rod Laver are among the few left-handed champions. Drobny defeated 19-year-old Ken Rosewall for the title.

The Rod Laver Touch

The boy was an unusual sight on the courts.

He was short and red-headed and often wore the comical floppy sun hat that Australians favor. He had a pinched, beak-nosed face. As he played, he chewed his lip or looked grim.

But oh, how he played. Left-handed!

The famous Australian coach, Harry Hopman, was dismayed when he first saw Rod Laver. "My, he's a little one," he said. "We'll have to do something about that sunken chest."

But the boy's nickname was "Rocket" because of his scorching serves. His returns were even better. He was a ferocious attacker, glaring with concentration as he whacked home winner after winner.

Skinny little Rod Laver went to Wimbledon in 1959. He lost that year, and in 1960, too. But the next year, after losing the Australian title, he won Wimbledon. His match against America's Chuck McKinley lasted only 55 minutes, the shortest since Jack Kramer's 45-minute victory in 1947.

In 1962, Rod was in fantastic form. He won the Australian championship and the Italian and French titles.

At Wimbledon, he was once again the Marvelous Mechanical Man. His spin shot on the backhand

Rod Laver of Australia became the second man ever to make a Grand Slam in tennis.

was like a cannonball. He defeated Martin Mulligan and took the Men's Singles — third leg of the Grand Slam.

No one had swept the Australian, French, English, and American titles since Don Budge in 1938. That was the year Rod Laver was born in Australia.

At Forest in 1962, Laver played the finals against his countryman, Roy Emerson. Emerson was to win Wimbledon in 1964 and 1965. The previous year, he had beaten Laver at Forest Hills in three sets.

But this year, the little redhead prevailed. Rod Laver won, 6-2, 6-4, 5-7, 6-4. The Grand Slam of tennis was his.

A famous tennis player came up from the audience to congratulate him. "If anyone ever deserved winning the Grand Slam, Rod Laver certainly deserved it. I was lucky in not having to compete against him."

The tennis player was Don Budge.

Laver turned pro the next year and thought he would never play at Wimbledon again. The famous tournament had always prided itself on its "pure" amateur status. Pro tennis players, who openly took money, were not considered fit to play with gentlemen.

All that went down the drain in 1968. In a last, shocking move, Wimbledon was declared an "open" competition. Pros and amateurs alike were allowed to play. Rod Laver returned and won the Men's Singles in 1968 and 1969. And in 1971, he won the Men's Doubles with his old friend and foe, Roy Emerson.

Two Girls From Australia

Until the 1960's, Australia had never had a great woman tennis player. Then Margaret Smith appeared on the world tennis scene. They called her "Big Margaret" because she was 5 feet 9 inches tall. She is perhaps the most powerful woman ever to play the game.

When Margaret Smith was a teen-ager, she was very skinny. She lifted weights to build up her muscles. When she was 17, in 1960, she won the Australian Women's Singles championship. Top-seeded at Wimbledon in 1961, she lost when her nerve failed.

Next year, she won the women's titles in France, Italy, and the United States. She was ranked first, but she lost in the first round to Billie Jean Moffitt (later King). Never before had the top seed been put away so quickly.

She was under enormous pressure to win in 1963. Margaret faced Billie Jean Moffitt in the finals. The big girl from Australia took an early lead, 6-3. But in the second set, Billie Jean rallied and went ahead, 4-2.

Margaret was known to choke under pressure. It was her most serious flaw. But she pulled herself together and volleyed into one corner. With all her strength, she sent the ball rocketing over the net, overpowering King. One last smash gave her the Singles title. She was the first Australian woman to win Wimbledon. She would win again in 1965 and 1970. In the latter year she became the second

woman to achieve a Grand Slam.

Evonne Goolagong was part-Aborigional. In her veins flowed the blood of the ancient people of Australia, the Stone-Age hunters that some scientists called the most ancient people on earth.

Evonne's parents were not wild bushmen. Her father was a sheep-shearer who made a modest living in the quiet country town of Barellan. The Goolagong family lived just like the other citizens. And like most Australian children, the little Goola-gongs played tennis in the local courts.

Shy Evonne won her first tournament when she was only ten. A famous coach, Vic Edwards, guided her career. In 1970, Evonne Goolagong went to Wimbledon for the first time. She was knocked out in the second round.

Next year, Evonne upset Margaret Smith Court in an Australian tournament. Goolagong had long admired the older woman. Mrs. Court said she would retire after 1971. Meanwhile, she promised to help Evonne.

At Wimbledon in 1971, Goolagong charmed everyone with her sunny smile. The crowd expected tennis players to be solemn — but here was Evonne, cheery as a bird. To everyone's surprise, she beat Billie Jean King in the semis. In the finals, her graceful baseline game made a hash of Margaret's power thrusts.

Evonne Goolagong crushed Margaret Smith Court, 6-4, 6-1. And Australia had its second great woman champion.

Evonne Goolagong, as unspoiled as she is charming and competent, is one of the two top Australian women players.

The Big Service

"Serve and volley." That was the Australian way of playing tennis — most of the time. And for 16 years, a parade of bronzed young men from Down Under dominated the Men's Singles at Wimbledon. Their names were Lew Hoad, Ashley Cooper, Neale Fraser, Rod Laver, Roy Emerson — and the last of the Big Serve Australians, John Newcombe.

During the time between 1956 and 1971, only three non-Aussies managed to take the men's crown. Alex Olmedo, born in Peru, won in 1959. Chuck McKinley of St. Louis won in 1963. And Manuel Santana of Spain took the title in 1966.

All of the Australians — except Rod Laver — used a very similar game. Power and attack! It was a style that many found boring because it was so overwhelming and lacking in color. But how those Aussies did bring home the hardware.

Sadly enough, this period was one of decline for tennis. The public began to lose interest in the game during the '60's. For one thing, people had more money. They wanted to participate in sports themselves rather than watch others play. Tennis lacked the violence of team games and there seemed to be little excitement in it. Furthermore, many people decided they would rather play the game themselves than watch others play.

Tireless young John Newcombe steps high as he returns the ball during 1967 Wimbledon play.

Also, the '60's were noted for the great pro-*versus*-amateur tennis flap. The best players wanted to earn a living playing the game. But if they turned pro, they would be barred from the major tournaments. A lot of tennis fans thought this was unfair. They wanted tournaments such as Wimbledon to feature the *best* players — whether they happened to be pro or amateur.

After the coming of open tennis at Wimbledon, crafty Rod Laver broke John Newcombe's Big Service and took the 1969 crown.

The next year, Newcombe faced veteran Ken Rosewall in the finals. Rosewall was a defensive specialist with a lightning backhand and a delicate touch. The crowd wanted him to win. But Newcombe won in five sets.

As the '70's began, the fortunes of tennis rose. Bringing in the pros had made all the difference. Attendance at matches soared. Most of the color still belonged to the women's contests. But men were turning back to the all-court game, too. The last of the Big Service champions was to be America's Stan Smith. After losing the finals to Newcombe in 1971, Smith won in 1972.

Defeated in the quarter-finals that year was a young man who would represent the wave of the future. He used a double-fisted backhand that was both weird and wonderful. His name was Jimmy Connors.

Queen Billie Jean

Tennis has not always been a popular sport in the United States. Throughout most of its history, it has been a game played by the rich and watched by the rich. After World War II, when large numbers of middle-class and lower-class young people began going to college, tennis players came from more modest backgrounds. But the fans were still mostly upper-class.

This happened because American tournaments were held in private clubs. Most of those who watched were members and guests. Tennis tournaments were seldom put on TV because most sports fans weren't interested.

One person changed all that—Billie Jean King.

She didn't seem like a world-beater when she began her career. Billie Jean Moffitt was not wealthy. Her father was a fireman in Long Beach, California. In 1955 when she was 11, Billie Jean played in her first tournament. Because she wore shorts instead of a dress, the tournament officials would not let her have her picture taken with the rest of the young players. It lit a spark in Billie Jean that would grow into an inferno. She would protest the many stuffy rules that limited tennis, and also discrimination against women — both as players and as human beings.

Billie Jean Moffitt first played at Wimbledon in 1961. In a surprise upset, she and her friend, Karen Hantze, won the Women's Doubles. The next year, she upset top-seeded Margaret Smith. Karen Hantze Susman won the finals, but the British press praised

"Little Miss Moffitt" as a future champion.

In 1963 and 1964, she was beaten by Margaret Smith. Then she studied under the Australian coach Mervyn Rose, who rebuilt her weak forehand and gave her a powerful new service.

In 1965, she went to Wimbledon again, after having married Larry King. She reached the semifinals, only to lose to Brazil's Maria Bueno — who bowed in turn to Margaret Smith.

The next year, Billie Jean King met Miss Bueno in the finals. She upset the three-time champion, 6-3, 3-6, 6-1. The King had become a queen.

In 1967, Billie Jean beat Maria Bueno again for her second Wimbledon title. She also won the American championship at Forest Hills.

As the top-ranked woman player, she felt she could now afford to speak out against what she felt were injustices. She called for tennis organizations to give up the old-fashioned rules that were smothering the game — the clothes rules, the rules against the gallery making any noise except polite applause, the holding of tournaments in private clubs that kept most of the public away.

Even more shocking, she called amateurism in tennis a sham. So-called "amateurs" had to take money under the table in order to make a living. Billie Jean said it was time that tennis players admitted they were *all* pros.

The old tennis order was slowly melting away. Pros began playing at Wimbledon in 1968. Billie Jean turned professional and won her third world title in a row.

Then she began speaking out for equal prize money for women players. All of this got her a lot of publicity. People who had never heard of other players — male or female — knew about Billie Jean King.

Knee trouble helped defeat her in the 1969 Wimbledon. Next year she was fit, but she lost the title to Margaret Smith in the longest women's match ever played, 14-12, 11-9.

In 1972, Wimbledon fans were rooting for Evonne Goolagong or for the young American, Chris Evert. They did not like Billie Jean any more. Her outspoken manner was not properly modest.

But King beat Goolagong, who had won the previous year. And in 1973, Billie Jean beat Chris Evert for her fifth Wimbledon title.

Later that year, she played her famous match against Bobby Riggs, who had said that women players did not deserve equal prize money because they were not as good as men. Billie Jean did not deny that the *best* male players could beat the best women. Men were naturally stronger. But she was furious when powerful Margaret Court let herself be psyched out by Riggs, a 55-year-old has-been.

Although few people expected her to win, Billie Jean herself was full of confidence. She crushed Bobby in three sets. Then she said, "I proved my point."

Billie Jean King in action at Wimbledon in 1974.
She lost in an early round to Russia's Olga
Morozova.

Love Match

It all happened so quickly.

Suddenly there were pro tennis *teams*. The top tournaments were televised all over the world. More people were playing and more people were watching tennis than at any time in history.

And in a climax almost too cute to be real, two young Americans, sweethearts engaged to be married, took the Men's and Women's Singles at Wimbledon.

Chris Evert had become famous at the age of 16, in 1971. She helped America beat Britain in the Wightman Cup tournament. She made a big hit at Forest Hills the same year. Fans liked her youth and beauty, her two-handed backhand, her coolness

Chris Evert gives Jimmy Connors a kiss after they won the 1974 Singles titles.

under pessure. They called her "the Ice Princess."

Wimbledon followers were eager to see a match between the two best young women players — Evert and Goolagong. The two met in 1972 in the semi-finals. Chris won the first set, 6-4, but Evonne took the second, 6-3, by hitting short to Chris's backhand. In the third set, they went to an exciting 4-4. Then Evonne broke Chris to take the set and the match.

In 1973, Chris reached the finals, but lost to Billie Jean King. Meanwhile, she had become engaged to another rising young American player, Jimmy Connors. He had great talent and like Chris, used a double-fisted backhand. Unlike her, he was cocky and made enemies by refusing to play on America's Davis Cup team. Too short for the Big Service, he made up for his lack of power by being agile and surprising.

By the time the 1974 Wimbledon rolled around, both Jimmy Conners and Chris Evert were in top form. While the world watched fondly, the two young folks — aged 21 and 19 — ripped up the sacred turf.

Chris defeated her Russian doubles partner, Olga Morozova, 6-0, 6-4. A day later, Jimmy met Ken Rosewall, now 39 and still trying for an elusive world title. Although most of the fans rooted for Rosewall, the American beat the Australian veteran, 6-1, 6-1, 6-4.

Then Chris and Jimmy posed together with their trophies. And a new, youthful era had come to the oldest tennis tournament of all, Wimbledon.

Jimmy Connors at Wimbledon in 1974.

Wimbledon Singles Champions

Men's Singles

1877	Spencer W. Gore
1878	P. F. Hadow
1879	J. T. Hartley
1880	J. T. Hartley
1881	William Renshaw
1882	William Renshaw
1883	William Renshaw
1884	William Renshaw
1885	William Renshaw
1886	William Renshaw
1887	H. F. Lawford
1888	Ernest Renshaw
1889	William Renshaw
1890	W. J. Hamilton
1891	Wilfred Baddeley
1892	Wilfred Baddeley
1893	Joshua Pim
1894	Joshua Pim
1895	Wilfred Baddeley
1896	H. S. Mahoney
1897	Reggie F. Doherty
1898	Reggie F. Doherty
1899	Reggie F. Doherty
1900	Reggie F. Doherty
1901	Arthur W. Gore
1902	H. Laurie Doherty
1903	H. Laurie Doherty
1904	H. Laurie Doherty
1905	H. Laurie Doherty
1906	H. Laurie Doherty
1907	Norman E. Brookes
1908	Arthur W. Gore
1909	Arthur W. Gore
1910	Anthony F. Wilding
1911	Anthony F. Wilding
1912	Anthony F. Wilding
1913	Anthony F. Wilding
1914	Norman E. Brookes
1915-18	NOT HELD
1919	Gerald L. Patterson
1920	William T. Tilden II
1921	William T. Tilden II
1922	Gerald L. Patterson
1923	William M. Johnston
1924	Jean Borotra
1925	Jean Rene Lacoste
1926	Jean Borotra

Women's Singles

1884	Maud Watson
1885	Maud Watson
1886	Blanche Bingley
1887	Lottie Dod
1888	Lottie Dod
1889	Blanche Bingley Hillyard
1890	L. Rice
1891	Lottie Dod
1892	Lottie Dod
1893	Lottie Dod
1894	Blanche Bingley Hillyard
1895	Charlotte Cooper
1896	Charlotte Cooper
1897	Blanche Bingley Hillyard
1898	Charlotte Cooper
1899	Blanche Bingley Hillyard
1900	Blanche Bingley Hillyard
1901	Charlotte Cooper Sterry
1902	M. E. Robb
1903	Dorothea Douglass
1904	Dorothea Douglass
1905	May Sutton
1906	Dorothea Douglass
1907	May Sutton

*OPEN COMPETITION

1908	Charlotte Cooper Sterry
1909	Dora Boothby
1910	Dorothea D. L. Chambers
1911	Dorothea D. L. Chambers
1912	E. W. T. Larcombe
1913	Dorothea D. L. Chambers
1914	Dorothea D. L. Chambers
1915-18	NOT HELD
1919	Suzanne Lenglen
1920	Suzanne Lenglen
1921	Suzanne Lenglen
1922	Suzanne Lenglen
1923	Suzanne Lenglen
1924	Kitty McKane
1925	Suzanne Lenglen
1926	Kitty McKane Godfree
1927	Helen Wills
1928	Helen Wills
1929	Helen Wills
1930	Helen Wills Moody
1931	Cilly Aussem
1932	Helen Wills Moody

1927	Henri Cochet
1928	Jean Rene Lacoste
1929	Henri Cochet
1930	William T. Tilden II
1931	Sidney Wood
1932	Ellesworth Vines
1933	Jack Crawford
1934	Fred J. Perry
1935	Fred J. Perry
1936	Fred J. Perry
1937	Donald Budge
1938	Donald Budge
1939	Bobby Riggs
1940-45	NOT HELD
1946	Yvon Petra
1947	Jack Kramer
1948	Bob Falkenburg
1949	Ted Schroeder
1950	Budge Patty
1951	Dick Savitt
1952	Frank Sedgman
1953	Vic Seixas
1954	Jaroslav Drobny
1955	Tony Trabert
1956	Lew Hoad
1957	Lew Hoad
1958	Ashley Cooper
1959	Alex Olmedo
1960	Neale Fraser
1961	Rod Laver
1962	Rod Laver
1963	Chuck McKinley
1964	Roy Emerson
1965	Roy Emerson
1966	Manuel Santana
1967	John Newcombe
1968*	Rod Laver
1969	Rod Laver
1970	John Newcombe
1971	John Newcombe
1972	Stan Smith
1973	Jan Kodes
1974	Jimmy Connors

1933	Helen Wills Moody
1934	Dorothy Round
1935	Helen Wills Moody
1936	Helen Jacobs
1937	Dorothy Round
1938	Helen Wills Moody
1939	Alice Marble
1940-45	NOT HELD
1946	Pauline Betz
1947	Margaret Osborne
1948	Louise Brough
1949	Louise Brough
1950	Louise Brough
1951	Doris Hart
1952	Maureen Connolly
1953	Maureen Connolly
1954	Maureen Connolly
1955	Louise Brough
1956	Shirley Fry
1957	Althea Gibson
1958	Althea Gibson
1959	Maria Bueno
1960	Maria Bueno
1961	Angela Mortimer
1962	Karen H. Susman
1963	Margaret Smith
1964	Maria Bueno
1965	Margaret Smith
1966	Billie Jean King
1967	Billie Jean King
1968*	Billie Jean King
1969	Ann H. Jones
1970	Margaret Smith Court
1971	Evonne Goolagong
1972	Billie Jean King
1973	Billie Jean King
1974	Chris Evert

SPORTS CLASSICS

WORLD SERIES
U.S. OPEN GOLF CHAMPIONSHIP
WIMBLEDON TENNIS TOURNAMENT
KENTUCKY DERBY
INDIANAPOLIS 500
OLYMPIC GAMES
SUPER BOWL
MASTERS TOURNAMENT OF GOLF
STANLEY CUP
NBA PLAYOFFS

CREATIVE EDUCATION